Original title:
Life's Great Question Mark

Copyright © 2025 Creative Arts Management OÜ
All rights reserved.

Author: Rory Fitzgerald
ISBN HARDBACK: 978-1-80566-207-5
ISBN PAPERBACK: 978-1-80566-502-1

Paradox of the Infinite

Why is the sky so very blue?
A mystery like why cats meow, too.
If I ask a fish about its fate,
Will it just swim around and wait?

Is time but a sandwich, neatly stacked?
Or a riddle that keeps us all intact?
When you ponder the shapes we all make,
Is it the question or the answer we bake?

Moments Between Answers

I asked the clock what makes it tick,
It laughed at me, then played a trick.
In moments of silence, we all try to think,
But the fridge hums loudly—what if we sink?

Answers are like socks, they hide and flee,
While we fumble about, hoping to see.
With questions alive like a bee in a jar,
Do we silence them all, or just raise the bar?

The Jigsaw of Existence

Each piece of the puzzle is wobbly and bright,
We force them together, oh what a sight!
Is the corner just shy, or has it misplaced?
Like trying to have a fun time, but still feel outpaced.

When all is assembled, there's still a space,
Why does it seem we can't find the grace?
Moments to crack the code on our chart,
Like chasing your thoughts that just won't depart.

What Lies Beyond the Horizon

Do clouds drink coffee or tea in the sky?
Are they pondering why the sun is so shy?
As I gaze out to where the blue meets the green,
Do they see off the edge where the laughter's unseen?

What if a bird could teach us to flow?
Would it tweet out the questions—the why and the whoa?
Maybe the wind knows what we're missing today,
But alas, it just giggles and sweeps us away.

Whispers of Uncertainty

In the depths of my mind, I ponder,
What's the deal with socks as a wander?
Do they roam while we're snoozing at night?
Finding joy in the laundry's delight.

Is there a manual for my daily spree?
Like a cat who's convinced he's a tree?
Questions dance like bees around flowers,
While I debate snacks for hours and hours.

In Search of Meaning

Why do we follow the same old route?
Is the corner shop really a hoot?
Or did I just walk into a plot,
Where every tomato has something to jot?

Is cereal really a soup in disguise?
I smile at the breakfast surprise.
If toast can pop, what's next on my list?
Maybe a pizza that's just been kissed.

Echoes of the Unknown

In the fridge, I hear a strange sound,
Is it leftovers trying to be found?
Or a pickle that dreams of a ride,
On a sandwich that's waiting with pride?

Do the plants gossip when I'm not around?
As they plot how to take back the ground?
Should I join in with their growing spree?
Or just stick to my couch, guilt-free?

The Space Between Thoughts

In the space where my thoughts take a break,
Do they dip in the pool of a giant cake?
Chatting quietly with the whispering breeze,
Or plotting to trick me with mismatched keys?

Is it normal to argue with my own shoe?
While my coffee insists it's still feeling blue?
They laugh while I chase my own crazy tail,
Collecting the tales of each hearty fail.

Footprints on an Unwritten Page

I stepped on thoughts that I can't trace,
But somehow find a witty face.
My chalk-dust dreams skip and sway,
In this odd dance of yesterday.

Each scribble laughed, a prankster's jest,
Could I be wrong? But who would guess?
With ink so bright on pages bare,
My nonsense rhymes float through the air.

Stars in the Twilight

In twilight's glow, the stars conspire,
To tease the moon and dance higher.
They wink and giggle, do they know?
What's up ahead, or just below?

I toss my wishes, catch a few,
What's next? A cow that jumps the blue?
As they twinkle with a cheeky grin,
Thoughts of what's next, where to begin?

The Loom of Possibility

With threads in hand, I weave a plot,
A tapestry of "Why not?"
Each color bright, a joke or two,
Stitching dreams, both strange and true.

The loom spins tales of silly schemes,
Like flying pies or talking beams.
In twists and turns, the laughter grows,
What's lost and found? Who really knows?

Roots of Contemplation

Beneath the ground, where thoughts take hold,
Roots twist and turn, both brave and bold.
They ponder why the sky is blue,
And chuckle at what trees would do.

With leafy whispers, secrets shared,
They plot and plan, but all is aired.
What wacky fruits will they produce?
A riddle wrapped in leafy juice?

Whispers of the Unanswered

Why does toast always land face down?
Cats seem to wear a constant frown.
Is the chicken just lost on its way?
Or do eggs have secrets they never display?

Why do socks vanish without a trace?
Never in pairs, they leave the race.
Is there a sock club that we can't see?
Or are they just plotting to be free?

Why do we park on driveways, I ask?
And in the yard, we must wear a mask?
Is it all part of a cosmic joke?
Or just the swirl of a cosmic poke?

Are we just characters in a play?
Jumping around in a silly ballet?
Why do we laugh, and then we weep?
Are we just thoughts in an endless sleep?

Shadows of Uncertainty

Is coffee just beans in a magic brew?
Or does it dance on toes we never knew?
How come my car always runs out of gas?
While I'm rushing for work, oh what a pass!

Why do ducks quack with such simple grace?
While humans trip on their own shoelace?
Do they hold secrets in their beak and waddle?
Or is it just fun, a silly dawdle?

Why do we sneeze when we smell a flower?
Is it the pollen or power of the hour?
Do donuts really bring happiness true?
Or is it just frosting that speaks to you?

Should we take life with a pinch of zest?
Dance like the mailman, always the best?
In this grand circus, let's play our parts,
With glorious laughter that fills our hearts!

The Curious Tapestry

Why do we call it a 'drive-thru' lane?
When we sit in our cars, waiting in pain?
Do the burgers gossip beyond the glass?
Or do fries just wish they'd all have class?

What's up with the socks that aren't a pair?
They sneak off to join a wider affair?
Are they attending a sock puppet show?
Or hiding away in a drawer, we'll never know?

Why do we dance when there's nobody near?
Creating our music, forgetting our fear?
Is it the rhythm that calls to us tight?
Or just our legs trying to take flight?

When life shows up with an awkward wink,
Do we fold our hands, or just stop to think?
Let's make the best of each riddle we face,
And laugh like the stars in a shimmering space!

In Search of the Elusive Why

Why do we poke at our phones all day?
Yet ignore the clouds drifting away?
Is the universe hiding the key to fun?
Or is it packed up, ready to run?

Why does ice cream melt in the sun's warm rays?
Skipping off with a grin, in so many ways?
Do flavors have tales they long to unfold?
Or are they just hungry for stories retold?

What's the deal with cats and their naps?
Do they dream of world domination maps?
Or are they just sneaking in a sweet snooze?
While plotting how best to confuse and amuse?

Are we just wanderers on this odd race?
With questions galore and a quirky grace?
Let's throw on our hats, join in the dance,
And giggle at life's perfect little chance!

Echoes of a Silent Inquiry

Why are we here, do you know,
With socks that never match or glow?
The cat thinks he's the great wise sage,
While we pretend to act our age.

We search for meaning in our cereal,
All while watching a sitcom material.
Is it in the fridge or in the sky?
Or found in that last slice of pie?

The birds chirp secrets we can't decipher,
While we chase laughter, hoping for a cipher.
Each tick-tock asks what we cannot see,
Like why do we keep losing our keys?

In the end, we chuckle and shrug,
Sipping tea, feeling quite snug.
With a wink at the chaos we've drawn,
We dance like fools until the dawn.

Threads of Unresolved Mysteries

What's the deal with missing remote,
Always playing a sneaky note?
The dog looks at me, eyes of a sage,
While I'm stuck reading some old page.

Why do socks vanish into thin air,
Leaving fashion a bold but bare affair?
I ponder my fate as I trip on the floor,
And wonder if I'd fit 'under one more.'

Do staplers have a secret pact,
Or do friends just like to distract?
The fridge hums softly; it has to know,
Why time flies faster than wobbly dough.

As questions bubble like a soda pop,
I float on whims, I won't stop.
For in this dance of thoughts and jest,
I find my humor, truly the best!

Navigating the Unknown

Is there a map for this crazy ride,
Or just a compass with broken pride?
I try to focus, but it's all a mess,
Even Google can't answer my quest.

The coffee spills, the toast burns black,
While I wonder if I'll ever get on track.
Why do things break when I'm in a rush?
Is the universe just having a crush?

With friends like these, who needs a guide?
We laugh at the chaos, take it in stride.
We chase the sunset, while dodging the rain,
Taking bets on where we'll go next, insane.

So here's to the path we wander down,
With giggles and fumbles, without a frown.
Through giggles and gasps, we find our way,
Laughing at questions, come what may.

The Quest for Hidden Truths

Why does the toaster pop with a grin,
Each time I insert bread, waiting to win?
Does it know secrets I can't unlock,
Or is it just playing a practical joke?

While the laundry spins tales of its own,
I chuckle at guessing, with less than I've known.
Is there wisdom in wrinkles or crumbs,
Or are we just dust, where knowledge comes?

What's the meaning of that odd flavor?
Like why does avocado act like a savior?
With awkwardness in every bite we take,
Are we on a quest for our own belly's sake?

As questions flutter, like leaves in the breeze,
We share a laugh, with guts like cheese.
In this merry chase, the truth may hide,
But with friends around, there's nothing to bide.

The Art of Unknowing

What's that itch behind my ear?
Is it wisdom or just a smear?
I ponder deep but then I laugh,
As I step on my own shoelace half.

Chasing thoughts like a runaway cat,
I swing and miss, that's where I'm at.
Details murky, like soup gone cold,
Unraveling stories never told.

Mirrors of the Mind

In a mirror, I see a face,
Where questions dance and thoughts embrace.
Do I really need to know it all?
I trip on riddles, stumble, and fall.

Reflections giggle, they know my name,
They whisper secrets, poke fun, and game.
Who's the fool? That's me, I guess,
Wrestling with thoughts in a playful mess.

Beneath the Ink of Time

Pages turn, but what's the plot?
Chapters jumbled, I've lost the spot.
Do I write a tale or doodle a line?
Between smiles, I sip my poetic wine.

The ink spills like laughter in the air,
What's true and what's just my hair?
I scribble nonsense in a joyful spree,
Seeking sense in the chaos of me.

An Odyssey of Intrigue

Set sail on a boat made of dreams,
Navigating thoughts that burst at the seams.
Is the treasure gold or just shiny fluff?
With every wave, I say, "That's enough!"

Mermaids laugh and sing out loud,
While I fumble, lost in the crowd.
An odyssey? Maybe just a walk,
Turning confusion into a joker's talk.

The Threads of Fate

In the web of choices, we often stray,
A sock goes missing, what can I say?
Should I wear blue or should I wear red?
The answers I seek are way over my head.

With noodles of fate that twist and twirl,
I grab at the straws, give time a whirl.
Is it too late to get my act right?
Did I just trip over my own online flight?

Coffee or tea? Will I need a mood lift?
Should I call my boss or just draft a gift?
Life's great puzzle is missing a piece,
Hiding in shadows, it tends to tease.

So here I dance on this tightrope of quirk,
Smiling at fortunes that tease and lurk.
Each silly mishap a chuckle or two,
In the game of surprises, I play peekaboo!

The Embrace of Mystery

In twilight's glow, we tread a fine line,
Fumbling with riddles as if they were wine.
Should I wear stripes with polka dots neat?
Fashioning chaos, oh what a treat!

Why is the cake always calling my name?
With forks as my allies, I play this strange game.
Is there magic in laughter, a tickle of chance?
Or is it just sugar that makes me do dance?

I ask the wind for wisdom and jest,
It whispers sweet secrets, but leaves me perplexed.
Where do socks go in the dryer's embrace?
Is there a portal to some other place?

As shadows emerge in this riddle of night,
I toast to the chaos, my silly delight.
With every twist, a giggle or sigh,
In the grand cosmic joke, I'll always comply!

In the Labyrinth of Thought

In the maze of my mind, I ponder,
Where's the exit? I yonder.
Chasing ideas that tease,
Like cats on a breeze.

I took a left, then a right,
What is wrong with this sight?
Thoughts knot like shoelaces,
In these dizzying places.

With each turn, a giggle grows,
Am I lost? Well, who knows?
A signpost with no clue,
Says 'Think more, and more too!'

Finally, I laugh, so sound,
In this madness, joy's found.
Though questions swirl like soup,
It's one heck of a loop!

Whirlwinds of Reflection

Spinning thoughts in a storm's eye,
Why do I always ask why?
Round and round, I go fast,
In the whirlwind, questions cast.

Is this a mirror or glass?
I just stumbled on the mass.
Reflections that make me grin,
Are these answers or just din?

Laughter rises with each twist,
So much humor I can't resist.
I ponder things like why socks fade,
In this comedy parade.

In the eye of this whirlwind spree,
I find a silly side of me.
With a chuckle and a twirl,
Life's a dance, give it a whirl!

Between Silence and Sound

In the quiet, thoughts collide,
Crazy questions, I can't hide.
A tap dance on my brain's floor,
Is that silence? Not anymore!

The whispers tease like a cat,
"Where's the truth?" they say and chat.
A ruckus in my head so loud,
I'm lost here, yet oddly proud.

Between echoes and stolen sighs,
I hear giggles, what a surprise!
Finding joy in the confusion,
A symphony of intrusion.

So let the noise distinctly roar,
In the chaos, I'll explore.
In silence or in sound, it's true,
Questions shine, like morning dew!

Riddles Beneath the Stars

Gazing up at glittered skies,
With questions dancing in my eyes.
What's a star's favorite joke?
"Twinkle, twinkle!" says its cloak.

A riddle wrapped in starlight's glow,
Why do wishes flow so slow?
My heart laughs with every guess,
In this sparkly, cosmic mess.

Comets race with witty flair,
"Do they travel? Do they care?"
Secrets whispered on the breeze,
With every cackle, worries freeze.

So beneath this velvet dome,
I find delight, I feel at home.
For in these riddles, there's a spark,
Life's riddles shine, like glowing arc!

Musings on the Edge of Wonder

In the morning light, I muse,
What's the point of a duck's yellow shoes?
Do they waddle for style or slip in the dew?
Maybe it's fashion, a quack-tastic view!

When clouds are made of cotton candy,
Is it okay to be a tad dandy?
Do squirrels write plays while frolicking trees?
Or are they just plotting to steal from me?

Do time travelers get awkward stares,
When they can't find the right pair of lairs?
Should I pack a snack for a trip through the past?
Or is a time warp just a diet blast?

Oh, what's the deal with socks and their match?
Are they hiding out, playing a game of catch?
If a shoe's in a corner, is it feeling blue?
Or dreaming of strolling in sunshine anew?

The Spectrum of Unasked Questions

When the moon wears a veil, does it hide its face?
Is it shy from the stars, longing for space?
Do jellybeans sing when they're left in the jar?
Or throw wild parties, dreaming of candy bars?

If laughter could float, would it ride on a breeze?
Would it tickle the trees, and charm all the bees?
Do flamingos ponder the color of pink?
Or just stand around, sipping drinks and to think?

Do umbrellas envy the sun's golden rays?
Or dream of the beach on their rainy days?
When the toast pops up, does it feel like a star?
Or just sit there waiting for butter and jam?

Can a cactus ever get lonely and blue?
Or does it just thrive with its prickles in view?
If wishes were kittens, would they nap in your lap?
Or chase after thoughts in an endless, warm nap?

Through the Veil of the Unseen

What if trees whispered secrets at night?
Would owls roll their eyes in a feathered fright?
Can a snail win a race if it dreams really hard?
Or is it just taking the slowest of cards?

Do mirrors have feelings when we glance their way?
Do they judge our reflection, or dance in dismay?
Is there a realm where lost socks come to play?
Or is it a riddle that leads us astray?

Can time on a calendar play hide and seek?
Does it laugh at us mortals, all frantic and weak?
If shadows could dance, would they trip on their feet?
Or sway like the leaves in a musical beat?

Do crayons have dreams of escaping the box?
Plotting the colors they'll use with their flocks?
If watermelons wore the crown of the fruit,
Would they reign supreme, or just know how to scoot?

The Canvas of Possibilities

If butterflies have wings made of frosting,
Do they flit to the bakery, never exhausting?
When rainbows decide to take breaks for a snack,
Do they munch on the clouds, or just take a hack?

When tadpoles dream of the frogs they might become,
Do they plot their big leaps, or just hum a drum?
Can cheese be so bold, it asks for a bit?
Or is it just shy, like a good little wit?

If the moon were to fall, would it bounce like a ball?
Or roll down a hill, have a cosmic freefall?
When shadows get tired, where do they go?
To nap under stars, or just take it slow?

If the sun wore a hat, what style would it choose?
A fedora or beanie, a grand hat with views?
Do giggles get lost in the heart of the cheer?
Or swim through the laughter, holding on near?

Shadows of Contemplation

Why does my cat stare at the wall?
Is there a ghost or just a fly at all?
I ponder deep while snacking on a pie,
Tangled thoughts that stretch to the sky.

Is this all a dream or just a show?
Why do socks vanish? Where do they go?
The kettle whistles, a spout of steam,
And I'm left wondering, was it all just a meme?

When is dinner ready? I think, I think!
Was it macaroni or shrimp that I planned to sink?
Spinning in circles like a crazed old hen,
I question it all, then repeat it again.

Beneath these shades, I try to unwind,
The cosmic joke is one-of-a-kind.
Yet with a chuckle, I pour out some tea,
And leave the mysteries, whatever they be.

Wandering Among the Wonders

There's magic in the way that beans grow tall,
In a pot they dance, have a ball,
Should I water them or sing a song?
Does a veggie garden really need to get along?

Puppies chasing tails in the sunny park,
Is it a quest or just a whimsical lark?
Each bark and wag asks questions profound,
While I ponder the meaning of life all around.

I bought a map, but lost my way,
Do I need directions for play today?
A sign says 'this way' but it feels a bit off,
Like trying to figure out a cat's very soft scoff.

The stars above twinkle, yes, it's quite grand,
But if I ask too many, will time disband?
I'll laugh and wander, taking it light,
In the land of the curious, just out of sight.

Tides of Inquiry

The ocean waves crash with questions untold,
Are they secrets from fish or mysteries old?
I need a snorkel to dive in and explore,
But what if I find a sock on the ocean floor?

Do tides have thoughts? Do they choose to rise?
Is there a current where wisdom lies?
I surf the waves and catch summer's zest,
While pondering if crabs ever take a rest.

As I build my castle, the tide pulls it back,
Is it an architect's joke or a cosmic hack?
I chuckle at seashells, each one a story,
But wonder if they all feel a bit hoary.

Swirling conundrums in salty wish pools,
Sometimes it feels like I'm swimming with fools.
Yet I splash and I play, with questions like foam,
In the dance of the ocean, I find a home.

Veils of the Unseen

What's behind the curtain where shadows dance?
A rubber chicken, perhaps? Or a strange romance?
My cat seems to know but just plays coy,
As I peer through the drapes like a curious boy.

The fridge hums secrets late at night,
Is it plotting a snack or a culinary fight?
I open the door, and all I receive,
Is a wilted carrot that once did believe.

Mirrors reflect more than just my face,
What if they're portals to a wild place?
A land where socks don't disappear each day,
And pizza is served in a magical way.

So I laugh at these veils, thin as a thread,
Tangled in humor, I dance instead.
With mysteries tucked in a quirky embrace,
I live with a wink, exploring the space.

The Puzzle of the Ineffable

In a box so tightly packed,
Lies a riddle, code intact.
I twist and turn, a fidgety guy,
Just to know, oh me, oh my!

Pieces jump as if they play,
Each corner asks, 'What's my say?'
Chasing answers like a cat,
Ignoring that there's no 'that'!

A jigsaw done upside down,
Turns my frown to a funny clown.
A moment of clarity, brief and bright,
Leaves me puzzled late at night!

With laughter as my guiding star,
I trip on puzzles, near and far.
What's the meaning? Who can tell?
I just found my missing shell!

Reflections in a Foggy Mirror

I stare into a foggy glass,
Where reflections twist and then bypass.
Is that my hair or a runaway mop?
In this riddle, I can't stop!

Who's the stranger with a hat?
Dare I ask him, 'What's up with that?'
Each smudge a question, a playful tease,
Like a matchmaker for laughs, if you please!

As I try to clear the view,
My toothbrush sports a morning dew.
Wiping thoughts through cloudy fumé,
I ponder, is this bright or gloomé?

Each spritz of cleaner, a chance to see,
Who's the funniest, them or me?
Oh, the mirror laughs so sly,
It hints that we're all a bit shy!

The Labyrinth of Thoughts

In a maze built from my own mind,
I wander round, what will I find?
Each turn a giggle, a silly hop,
As thoughts do tango, twirl, and drop!

I meet a rabbit wearing a hat,
He grins at me, says, 'How 'bout that?'
With each strange twist, I start to roam,
Wondering if I'll find my home.

A signpost reads, 'Choose A or B,'
I pick both, cause they're both funny!
Lost in laughter, I just can't care,
Each dead end's a joke laid bare!

With my brain's compass all askew,
I dance with thoughts that feel brand new.
In this maze of whimsy and plight,
It turns out wrongs can feel quite right!

Constellations of Wondering

Stars scribble notes up in the night,
Are they laughing? Oh, what a sight!
Each twinkle's a wink, a wink from up there,
Inviting me to join in their flair!

The Milky Way whispers tales so grand,
Of ducks with hats and a pizza stand.
Orbiting dreams like it's a big joke,
Who knew stardust wrote ads for folk?

Planets collide with a crash and a pop,
They giggle and glide, never want to stop.
"Who am I?" I ponder as they dance,
What if I'm just part of their prance?

With laughter pulling me through every star,
I think I'm a piece of their bazaar.
In the cosmos, we all take flight,
Chasing wonders that feel just right!

The Unfolding Paradox

I woke up today feeling quite bright,
But my coffee's gone cold, what a fright!
I ponder my socks; one's black, one's blue,
Is it fashion or chaos? I haven't a clue.

The cat's on the roof, and the dog's chasing flies,
While I'm here debating the length of my ties.
Should I dance in the rain or just stay inside?
With all of these choices, I'm tongue-tied!

I tried counting blessings; I lost track at six,
Now I'm juggling lemons, oh what a mix!
With gravity teasing, I tumble and fall,
And wonder if tripping counts after all.

So here I am laughing, a lovely charade,
Finding my joy in this grand masquerade.
For life's just a puzzle with pieces askew,
A hilarious game, is it not? Yes, it's true!

Fables of the Uncharted

In a world where the green ducks wear hats of the sun,
And squirrels debate which pancake's more fun,
The roads untraveled stretch far and wide,
Yet I end up here with my pet snail as guide.

Oh, the stories we share on our brave little quest,
Is it better with chocolate? That's anyone's guess!
And what if the moon is just cheese on a plate?
Should we dine with the stars before it gets late?

With each quirky twist comes a voice that won't hush,
Should I dance with a cactus or simply just blush?
A jester may laugh, while the wise shake their head,
But I'll wear a crown of spaghetti instead.

So here in this riddle, we strut and we scheme,
Crafting fables of things that we hope are supreme.
In the wild woods of thought, I'm tripping and torn,
Yet every odd moment's a treasure reborn!

Chains of Possibility

I stood at a crossroads, scratched my dear head,
One path was for veggies, the other for bread.
With each step I pondered, what might come next,
A hiccup for sure; I'm not feeling perplexed!

A frog hops beside me, gives a sly grin,
He asks if I've thought of where to begin.
Should I leap into puddles and splash all around?
Or waltz with the shadows that dance on the ground?

Every new choice wears a silly disguise,
Like socks on a parakeet, oh what a surprise!
To choose is to dance with both chaos and fate,
And sometimes it's golden to just be late.

So here I am musing on paths yet to tread,
With nachos for wisdom and pop tarts for bread.
Why choose just one doorway when free to explore?
Let's play in this maze; who could ask for more?

The Balance of Certainty

When the string beans yelled 'quite certain' at noon,
I laughed so hard I spun round like a cartoon.
Do I trust the recipe or mix by the whim?
With numbers and letters, my senses grow dim.

Yet the calendar chirps with a patient appeal,
Reminding me gently that time likes to steal.
Should I plan out my week or go with the flow?
With cookies as bribes, I'm ready to go!

In a whirl of decisions, I juggle and sway,
For logic's a dance, so I'm here for the play.
To find what I want, I might flip a coin,
And let it decide if I dance or if join.

So balance will guide me through this silly twist,
Where certainty mingles and sweet dreams exist.
In the riddle of choices, I chuckle and grin,
For every new challenge, I'm eager to win!

Chronicles of the Unsung

In the corner, heroes stew,
Chasing dreams and plenty of dew.
With capes made from bath towels tight,
They fight dust bunnies by night.

Their secret lair, a cluttered room,
Where dirty socks find their doom.
With laughter loud and pizza piles,
They solve the world's quirkiest miles.

Armed with nothing but a snack,
They plan to dance, not hold back.
With hopes high like popcorn on pop,
They'll conquer whims, no chance to stop.

So raise a toast to the uncrowned,
In their chaos, joy is found.
For every giggle, jest, and cheer,
The unsung heroes persevere!

Beneath the Surface of Existence

Do fish ponder what we think?
Beneath the waves, do they rethink?
While we humans sip our tea,
Are they debating: 'What's a sea?'

Fish hats swirl as they prance,
Creating currents with their dance.
With bubbles shared, they giggle wide,
Was that a whale, or just a tide?

Shall we build them treasure chests?
To hold their dreams and fishy quests?
Or just a sign that reads in jest:
"Eel-come to the scaly fest?"

So here's to the depths, both vast and deep,
Where fish debate and secrets keep.
For every splash brings timeless fun,
Beneath the surface, life's a pun!

When Silence Speaks

In quiet moments, whispers bloom,
A sock slips out of a vacuum's gloom.
As each tick echoes from the clock,
Does time giggle or just mock?

The potted plant slyly rolls an eye,
As the fridge hums a soft goodbye.
Is the couch judging our snacks so grand?
As crumbs do a victory dance unplanned?

When the cat stares, does he know?
The secrets of the world, in silent flow.
Does he ponder the neighbor's dog?
Or dream of ruling a log-shaped fog?

In silence lies the loudest jest,
As chaos swirls, and we find rest.
Let's toast to quiet and its shared quirks,
For in the hush, humor lurks!

Footprints on a Foggy Trail

Through misty pathways, we tread slow,
With soggy shoes and laughter glow.
Where did these footprints come from, friend?
Are they ours, or a stranger's blend?

Maybe it's Bigfoot trying to race,
In a sprint to win the human pace.
Or a goose in search of a crumby snack,
Leaving trails as it makes its track!

The fog rolls in—what shall we do?
Find a compass, or just follow you?
With giggles bouncing off the trees,
We'll wander where the laughter fleas.

So let's embrace the whimsy's call,
In fog, we might just find it all.
For every step and silly slide,
In mysteries, joy will forever abide!

The Embrace of Ambiguity

In a world wrapped in a riddle,
I ask if this is real or a fiddle.
Is my lunch a feast or a prank?
Who knew my sandwich had so much rank?

The fish swims left, the cat jumps right,
What is the meaning? I'll take a bite.
Do socks really die in the dryer?
Or are they just part of the choir?

Possibilities in the Mist

I woke up today with fizz in my head,
And a mischievous cat sneaking under my bed.
Are socks and spoons in a hidden affair?
Or is it just fluff that dances in air?

Coffee's a potion, it makes me a knight,
Though I still can't find my left from my right.
Should I wear polka dots or stripes instead?
Is it fashion or madness, or just all in my head?

Threads of the Infinite

In the fabric of what could be true,
Is my shoe on the right foot or two?
Is the universe silly or just a charade?
Do pancakes giggle, are muffins afraid?

The stars are confused, they wink and they twirl,
What if they're just in a cosmic whirl?
When the light bulb fizzles, what does it say?
Is it 'Stop pondering!' or 'Keep doubts at bay'?

The Dance of Inquiry

I pulled on a thought, it started to twirl,
As questions lined up, they began to swirl.
Are we all just players in a silly show?
Or simply balloons that forgot how to blow?

The chicken crossed roads with a wink and a smile,
Is it just for a joke or has she walked a mile?
Should I take the bus or just run with the breeze?
Perhaps I'll just sit and count all the trees!

Facets of the Human Heart

Have you ever lost a sock,
Only to find it's found another flock?
We've all got quirks, oh what a sight,
Like dancing with joy, then taking flight.

A heart is a puzzle, mixed and bizarre,
Like a cat that thinks it's a superstar.
One minute we giggle, the next we frown,
What's up with the tears when the clown's in town?

We hoard our secrets, tucked away tight,
Yet blurt them out in the middle of night.
With pizza in hand and ice cream near,
We ponder our dreams with a chuckle and cheer.

So raise up a glass to our quirkiest ways,
Where laughter and love light up our days.
Each twist and turn, as wild as a cart,
Is simply the charm of the human heart.

The Silence Between Us

There's a dance on the tip of the tongue,
While the clock ticks away and the coffee's unsung.
We're experts at silence, a peculiar game,
Where awkwardness sits—oh, what a shame!

You nod at my joke, though it's quite out of place,
And I stare at my shoes—what a heavenly space.
Our eyes do the talking, though lips stay sealed,
In this quiet confusion, we've both agreed.

Like two squirrels debating on who takes the nut,
We sit in this silence, each one in a rut.
It's a comedy show with no laugh track,
Yet here we are waiting, for ... maybe a snack?

So let's raise a glass to the pauses and waits,
To the shenanigans nested in friendships' gates.
For in the pauses, we're never all alone,
Just a funny little silence that's all our own.

Seeking the Spirals of Existence

In the quest for the meaning, we spin like a top,
Over coffee-stained maps, we'll never stop.
We chase after answers, like cats to a string,
But what we find first is an overly bold king.

Do we twirl in circles or dance in a line?
Each zig and each zag makes us feel just fine.
Yet every philosopher is lost in their thoughts,
While I'm stuck eating donuts, forgetting what's hot!

Count the stars and the socks, keep score of the fun,
It's a game of existence, and we all want to run.
We search for the spiral—it's quite an odd feat,
Like tumbleweed racing—oh, there goes my seat!

So grab me a donut, let's laugh at our plight,
As we ponder the spiral beneath the moonlight.
Each turn and each twist, a riddle to cheer,
With a sprinkle of joy, let's toast without fear!

Lanterns in a Darkened Wood

When shadows creep in like a sly, cheeky cat,
We wander through trees, being chased by a rat.
The lanterns we carry show way more than light,
They rescue our dreams from the depths of the night.

With every crackle of leaves under feet,
We giggle at ghosts that just can't take a seat.
The woods hold their secrets, sweet whispers abound,
As we trip on soft roots and tumble around.

Yet in the darkness, we're not alone here,
With lanterns that sparkle, we've nothing to fear.
So let's shimmy and sing 'neath the moon's silver glow,
For laughter and friendship make the best show!

So raise up your lantern, let's dance in the night,
In this darkened wood, everything feels just right.
Our lanterns keep shining, as we skip and we sway,
Illuminating joy in the silliest way.

Lines in the Sand

In the beach of thoughts, I drew a line,
With a squiggle here, it seemed just fine.
Sandcastles crumbled, my grand design,
The tide rolled in, oh well, divine!

Footprints fading, a comical race,
As I pondered deep, this sandy place.
But wait—who's that? It's my own face!
Laughing back at my silly chase.

A seagull squawked, like it could tell,
"What's this foolishness? You know so well."
I shrugged and winked, oh what the shell!
The universe giggled, all is swell!

As waves washed over, doubts in retreat,
I realized life's a mix of sweet and sweet.
With every wave, we take a seat,
In the comedy show, we can't be beat!

Conversations with the Void

I sat with the void, in a coffee shop,
"Tell me your secrets! Please don't stop!"
It just sat there, a real big flop,
Sipping silence, like fizzy pop.

I asked about purpose, it winked and quirked,
"Why so serious? Here, just lurked!"
It tossed me a donut, sweetened and perked,
In a world of chaos, we both smirked.

With metaphors swirling, we shared a grin,
"What is the meaning?" I tossed in the tin.
The void just shrugged, said, "We're all in.
Life's just a game, let's begin!"

So there we sat, void and me,
In laughter and queries, all laid free.
Who knew the emptiness could be so glee?
Banters with nothing, a life's jubilee!

Moments of Epiphany

One day I tripped over my own thought,
Should've seen it coming, it was fraught.
An epiphany hit! Like a sudden plot,
"Keep falling, you fool, the lessons are caught!"

Stumbling around with my shoes untied,
Every misstep became my guide.
I laughed at the folly, my ego fried,
Finding wisdom where I would abide.

On a café napkin, I scribbled a rhyme,
"Life's two left feet, but still worth the climb!"
A moment of clarity, sweet and sublime,
In the chaos, I found a rhythm and mime.

So here's to the stumbles, the slips, and the falls,
In the dance of existence, we answer the calls.
With each little trip, the laughter enthralls,
And joy wraps around us, like love's gentle walls!

The Eye of the Unfathomable

Peering deep into the cosmic stew,
I asked, "Hey there, what's the big view?"
A wink from a star, said, "Just be true,
The eye is wide, and so are you!"

I took a breath, feeling small but grand,
In this vastness, I tried to understand.
Such comical wonders, life's clumsy band,
Dancing 'round mysteries, we take a stand.

The unseeable giggled, "Got questions galore,
But ponder too long, and you'll just snore!"
So I played hopscotch on the cosmic floor,
Jumping through curiosities, wanting more!

And though I may not find all the clues,
I'll join the dance with the stars and their hues.
In a twirl of confusion, I gladly choose,
To laugh at the questions, and sometimes snooze!

The Colors of Wondering

Why's the sky so blue today?
Is it wearing denim or just play?
Birds can't spell the words they sing,
Do they know the joy they bring?

Clouds in shapes, a dog, a cat,
Do they giggle, imagine that!
Rainbows coming after rain,
Did they pack a colorful train?

Why do socks go missing fast?
Do they hide from us at last?
Puddles jump when kids go past,
Are they waiting for a splash?

Lollipops that twist and swirl,
Do they dance in candy whirl?
Whispers of the ice cream cone,
Is it lonely on its own?

A Canvas of Questions

Paint your dreams on watermelon slices,
Do they taste like sugary spices?
Why does summer breeze feel shy?
Does it tickle clouds floating by?

Why do cats take all the chairs?
Do they plan kitty affairs?
Is the moon full or just brave?
Does it hide in a marshmallow cave?

Why does popcorn jump so high?
Are they chasing the butterfly?
Do crayons scribble when they play?
What do they want to say today?

If the sun wore sunglasses bright,
Would it shine with more delight?
Do shadows whisper secrets deep?
Or do they just like silent sleep?

Reflections in a Crystal Pool

If the fish could ask for tea,
Would they prefer it with a spree?
Why do frogs leap with such cheer?
Are they bouncing dreams, I fear?

Why do we giggle at tickles too?
Does laughter taste like morning dew?
When daisies wave in the breeze,
Are they dancing to their own tease?

Do stars wear pajamas at night?
Or do they shimmer just for sight?
When shadows play, do they get shy?
Or do they just want to say hi?

Why does bread always fall face down?
Is it aiming for a frown?
Do toast and jam ever conspire?
For a breakfast filled with fire?

Searching for the Unsaid

Where do whispers often go?
Do they dance with a gentle flow?
Why do onions cause a cry?
Are they hiding their sweet reply?

Do shoes gossip when you're gone?
Or do they just play the dawn?
If clouds sneeze, what do we do?
Grab a coat, or wear a shoe?

If apples giggle when they fall,
Do they hope to bounce off the wall?
When popcorn pops, is it surprised?
Or just food that's mesmerized?

Why does butter melt with ease?
Does it join the dance of breeze?
When dreams escape on a slide,
Do they laugh, or just try to hide?

Tracing the Paths of Curiosity

Why is the sky blue, you ask?
Is it jeans on clouds, on some funny task?
Do fish wear glasses to see underwater?
Or do they laugh at us—what a big blunder!

We ponder the moon's cheesy delight,
Is it made of Gouda or just a great light?
Do ants hold debates on their tiny paths?
While we scratch our heads and split our laughs.

What do birds chat about on the wing?
Do they gossip 'bout squirrels and what they bring?
Maybe they're plotting to steal our souls,
With nuts in their pockets and clever goals!

At the end of the day, we still might sigh,
Wondering deeply why we even try.
But as we chuckle at thoughts so absurd,
The answers may come without a single word!

Shifting Sands of Understanding

Why do we trip on the things we can't see?
Like socks in the dryer, where could they be?
Do camels laugh at our silly shoes?
Or are they just glad they never lose?

Every grain in the desert seems to talk,
Shifting and shuffling, a silent mock.
What if the sun has a playful side,
And plays tag with shadows that try to hide?

Do fish learn to swim before they are born?
What happens to hats when they just get worn?
Is there a tree that whispers the score?
Of all the odd things we just can't ignore?

So let's dance on the sand with a curious grin,
As we wonder about all that might have been.
With a chuckle here and a giggle there,
Maybe we'll find answers, lurking somewhere!

The Mystery of Every Dawn

As morning breaks, what's that glow?
Is it the sun saying, 'Hey, let's go!'?
Or is it toast popping, all golden brown?
And the cat's plotting how to steal my frown?

What do clouds whisper as they drift above?
Do they conspire 'bout the skies they love?
Are they just bored, or seeking a thrill?
Or play hide and seek, keeping us still?

Do roosters croak just to shock the sun?
Or is it their way of having some fun?
Each new day brings questions to chase,
Like why do we hurry; what's the big race?

As we sip our coffee, lost in thought,
The day ahead becomes the schemes we've sought.
With laughter echoing from each dawn's charm,
Maybe the mystery holds us warm!

Between Dreams and Realities

What's in a dream that feels so real?
A dancing giraffe or a spaghetti wheel?
Is that rain on my face, or just my cat?
Who knew the night could be so full of that?

Between what we wish and the thoughts that we weave,
There's a circus of wonders we can't conceive.
Do pillows judge us for how we rest?
While we play board games with our subconscious jest?

Do our socks run away on some grand quest?
Seeking adventure, or just taking a rest?
Every dream's a riddle, a whimsical play,
A mix of our thoughts from the day to sway.

So let's relish the blur of our daydreams wild,
As the mind dances free, like a curious child.
In the land of the funny, where laughter takes flight,
Is all that we want found between day and night?

Echoing Questions

Why does toast always land face down?
Is there a club for the awkward clown?
Do socks have secret parties at night?
And why do good plans always take flight?

What if cats are plotting our fate?
Do they laugh when we think they wait?
Is coffee actually a magic brew?
Or just a warm hug brewed just for you?

Can ducks ever be seen wearing hats?
Is there a business for chatty bats?
Are we the stars in someone's dream?
Or just the punchline of a cosmic meme?

When will time stop acting so fast?
And why do desserts never seem to last?
Is there a reason for all this fuss?
Maybe the secret's just to laugh with us!

The Bridge of Perception

Do fish ever wonder about the sky?
And do birds ever ask, 'Why don't I try?'
Is there a map to navigate thought?
Or just a riddle that can't be caught?

Why do shoes get lost in the dark?
And socks? They just run off to the park!
Can a chair ever get tired of sitting?
And who keeps the vase from just quitting?

What's with the cats and their stealthy ways?
They seem to plot in mysterious ways!
Is laughter the sound of the universe me?
Or just a way to be slightly less free?

When will we unlock the grand design?
Or is there really no finish line?
Perhaps we're all just pebbles in stream,
Laughing at life like it's just a dream.

Seasons of Unfolding

Why does spring feel like a chance to dance?
And summer says, 'Come take a chance!'
Is autumn truly nature's farewell?
Or just her way of casting a spell?

Do winter coats dream of being free?
Or rave about warmth with a snooty glee?
Does every leaf make a wish on the breeze?
Or plot with the clouds, 'Let's tease the trees!'

What if time's just a recycle bin?
Where moments go for a cheeky spin?
Can joy be bottled, or shared in a song?
Or is the madness where we all belong?

When will the seasons stop playing games?
Or will they keep dubbing us all with names?
Perhaps the magic lies in the ride,
With each twist and turn we can't help but glide!

The Archive of What If

What if I danced with a chicken today?
Would it cluck to the beat or lead me astray?
Do chairs daydream about being sat?
Or conspire, 'Let's all give that human a chat!'

Is there a library of lost chances found?
Or do jokes get retired when they hit the ground?
Can a sandwich secretly want to be sushi?
Or will it stay bread and feel quite pushy?

What if colors had feelings, too?
Would blue be the calm, and red feel like glue?
Do puzzles roll their eyes at what we don't see?
Or laugh at us missing the 'key' to 'be'?

When will we laugh at our silly ways?
Or treasure the nonsense of all our days?
Maybe the wisdom is just being grand,
And shrugging at questions we don't understand!

Each Breath's Unspoken Query

Why do socks disappear, it's quite a feat,
They vanish when I wash, it's such a cheat.
Do they have a party, or start a new life?
While I just sit here, with my laundry strife.

Is cereal just soup in a morning bowl?
Are we just the leftovers of a big ol' soul?
Do plants ever wonder if they're just in style?
Growing with grace, or just for a smile?

What's the deal with cats, they sit and stare?
Do they ponder deep thoughts, or simply not care?
Every time they meow, is it a big con?
Or simply a ploy for the food that's gone?

In the end we giggle, as questions spin round,
With each silly thought, new wonders are found.
So let's toast to the quirks, the laughs we chance,
For every odd query, there's always a dance.

The Path of the Inquisitive Soul.

Why does toast always land butter-side down?
Is it plotting revenge on my breakfast crown?
Do toasters have grudges we'll never behold?
They laugh at our crumbs, oh, the stories they hold!

What's with the ducks that waddle in line?
Are they off to a meeting, sipping on wine?
With their quacks as the chatter, they strut with esteem,
Planning world domination, or so it would seem.

Are chairs secretly training for Olympic games?
Do they dream of the moment when no one remains?
As folks sit and ponder about life's funny tricks,
Do they whisper sweet nothings, or talk politics?

Oh, questions abound, like birds taking flight,
Each query we ask gives the brain a delight.
Let's chuckle together at thoughts that may roam,
With a giggle we gather, we're never alone.

Unraveled Queries

Why do we park in a driveway, yet drive on the street?
It's just one of those puzzles that can't be discreet.
Are keys really magic, or just shiny tools?
Making our doors open, while breaking the rules.

What's up with the weather, it's never the same?
One day it's sunshine, the next it's a rain game.
Do clouds get confused, or just play hide and seek?
They float on the breeze, while we peek and squeak.

Is spaghetti a noodle, or is it a worm?
Twisting, and twirling, in its saucy term.
Do forks have their own secret club in the drawer?
When we're not around, do they practice and soar?

In the chaos of queries, we giggle and cheer,
For every odd question, there's joy to endear.
So let's ponder these puzzles, with smiles so bright,
For every great query, brings laughter and light.

The Pause Between Heartbeats

Why does popcorn pop, it's quite a surprise?
Are kernels just waiting for their moment to rise?
With a sizzle and crackle, they leap in the air,
Turning simple snacks into bold culinary flair.

If a sneeze is a mini-explosion of sorts,
Is catching it in time our best sport of retorts?
Do we share in the laughter, or cover in shame?
Each sneeze is a scandal, but we're all the same.

Do fish in a tank have deep thoughts as they swim?
In bubbles and ripples, do they ponder or grin?
As we gaze at their antics, so carefree and spry,
Are they rolling their eyes at our questions, oh my!

With echoes of laughter, we set our minds free,
As we navigate questions like birds on the sea.
So let's relish the moments, and pause just a beat,
For every fun query turns dull days to sweet.

Unwritten Stories of Tomorrow

What will tomorrow bring our way?
Will it be sunshine or a rainy day?
A pizza on the table, or burnt toast,
Just waiting on the fridge for us to boast.

We plot our lives like a grand old play,
Yet end up lost in a silly ballet.
Should I wear socks or mismatched shoes?
The stars may know, but I'm just confused.

The cake I baked, a signal of glee,
Looked great on the outside, but wait, not for me!
With a twist of fate, it fell down flat,
My dog now cries, "What was up with that?"

So here's to tomorrow, a comic spree,
Chasing the unknown, wild and free!
With laughter and wit, we dance and rhyme,
And redefine the shapes of time.

A Realm of Wonder

In a land of socks that never pair,
Where lost keys dance in the midnight air,
I trip on dreams, explode with cheer,
While wondering if the fridge holds beer.

A cow jumps over the moon each night,
Fetching stardust with all its might.
Yet here I sit, just solving fables,
With breakfast choices like broken labels.

I asked a turtle to share its tale,
It said, "I'm slow, but I never fail."
Around the bend, a raccoon did peek,
"Why chase the cheese? Just take a leak!"

In this realm of quirks and goo,
Where all our oddities feel so true,
Let's twirl with visions, wild and grand,
And giggle together, hand in hand.

Seeking the Threads of Fate

What is the sauce that makes life sweet?
Is it the cookies that I sneak to eat?
Or searching for socks in a laundry war,
Only to find I've got one pair more?

I ponder if fate plays a game of chess,
While I lose my moves and then second guess.
A squirrel steals my fries from the patio,
And I scream, "Hey, that's my next video!"

The universe quips, maybe just chill,
Ask that cactus if it's got a thrill.
I could write novels or blow up balloons,
Maybe juggle life's ups and its swoons!

So here's to the threads we try to weave,
In these silly dreams, let's laugh and believe.
For in the madness, we find our place,
Seeking the threads with a smile on our face.

Beyond the Horizon of Knowing

What's over yonder, just beyond sight?
Could it be dancing cats in the moonlight?
Or maybe a pond where the fish wear hats,
Sipping on tea with some cultured rats?

We squint at the world, trying to find,
All of its puzzles that play with the mind.
I asked a llama what's under its charm,
It winked at me, then chewed on my arm!

Beyond knowing lies a land of jest,
Where giggles come first, and quizzes are best.
Do ducks know secrets that I can't divulge?
Or is it just me in this whimsical plunge?

So let's raise our cups to the dawn of surprise,
To the whims of adventure, and not being wise.
In laughter we find the great unknown,
With each inane thought, we've brightly grown.

Where Certainty Meets Curiosity

Why is the sky blue, one might ask?
The answer slips away, a funny task.
I tried to catch it with a net of thought,
It laughed and wiggled, now it can't be caught.

Do cats really know what we're up to?
I swear they conspire over our shoe!
With puzzled faces, they plot and scheme,
Stealing our snacks while we chase a dream.

Are fish in tanks the new mood rings?
Swirling around, they are royalty kings.
Bubbles burst forth with a giggle and splash,
While we ponder futures in a culinary bash.

When the clock strikes twelve, what happens then?
Do we turn into pumpkins or just back to men?
Tick-tock the questions bounce off the wall,
But who really knows? Let's just have a ball!

Dancing with Doubt's Embrace

Oh, to tango with thoughts in a comfy shoe,
Shuffling and sliding, but what's really true?
Do ducks fly south for the winter chill?
Or do they lounge on grass, just for the thrill?

There's a conga line of curious minds,
Twisting and turning, seeking all kinds.
What's up with socks that vanish, oh dear?
They must be on vacation, sipping cold beer!

Doubt wears a tutu, dancing so light,
Whirling through questions that scare us at night.
Do we ever land on solid ground?
Maybe we're just spinning around and around!

Let's Rumba with reasons and waltz with the what-ifs,
As we chase after answers, our brain's playful gifts.
Unraveling giggles, our hearts fill with cheer,
For the dance of uncertainty, we all hold dear.

The Unfolding of the Unknowable

In a world of mysteries twisted and curled,
We peek through the curtains to see the wild world.
Do rabbits know they can't wear a hat?
Although truly they'd look dapper—imagine that!

On the stage of the strange, the act goes on,
Juggling the chances like a wacky brawn.
Do clouds get tired from all that float?
Or are they just resting 'till it's time to gloat?

When questions sprout like weeds from the ground,
We water them lightly; answers are found.
Is toast really better with butter or jam?
Let's try both and channel our inner glam!

The telltale signs are all so bizarre,
Mismatched socks and a dancing guitar.
What's next on the list? We've got no clue,
But let's take a gamble, with breezy review!

Whims of Fate's Design

Fate tosses dice like a playful child,
Ants on a picnic are always so wild.
When biscuits fall, is it luck or chance?
Or are they just leading us into a dance?

Oh, what if spoons could fly like a bird?
Stirring up trouble, it seems quite absurd!
A fork's sharp wit and a knife's slick smile,
Their antics would keep us entertained for a while.

Who chose the names for the things we know?
Can we talk to chairs or food that won't grow?
What if broccoli shapes into dancing trees?
Would we cook them for dinner, or just let them freeze?

Fate giggles sweetly with her whimsical tunes,
As we ponder the universe under bright moons.
So let's crack a joke, with laughter to shine,
Embrace all the quirks in fate's grand design!

The Symphony of Unanswered

In the park, a duck does quack,
While pondering what's behind its back.
A breeze blows leaves, they dance and swirl,
Each twist and turn a playful twirl.

A cat sits still, so very wise,
Watching ants with curious eyes.
Do they know where they are bound?
Or do the questions bounce around?

A squirrel pauses, mid-scamper trace,
With a nut, as if it's a piece of grace.
It looks at us, then hides away,
Maybe pondering its nutty play.

The sun dips low, shadows grow long,
A chicken sings the day's last song.
As crickets chirp their nightly cheer,
Unanswered bliss is still so near.

Where Certainty Meets Chaos

In the morning, socks don't match,
My brain's a game of catch and hatch.
The coffee spills, begins a dance,
As if it's taking the day's chance.

A to-do list, so grand yet meek,
With doodles of dragons in a streak.
I check it twice, then lose my pen,
And wonder where it did all begin.

The cat jumps high to catch a fly,
Crashing down with a startled cry.
He wasn't sure, took quite a leap,
Now he ponders the world's deep sweep.

My plants ask for water, I pour with glee,
But half the time, they drown with me.
In chaos, there's a magic swirl,
As we all dance in a wobbly twirl.

Parables of Perplexity

A goldfish swims in a tiny bowl,
Wondering where it lost its soul.
With bubbles floating, thoughts arise,
Are they the answers or just lies?

A dog digs deep, as if to find,
The secrets of all humankind.
But all he finds is old lost bones,
A stash of treasures, not a throne.

The clock strikes twelve, fashionably late,
I question why we hesitate.
It runs in circles, round it goes,
Are we just pawns in time's grand show?

The mailman comes with tales to share,
Of far-off lands and wild affair.
Yet here I sit with my tea so hot,
Perplexed by things that matter not.

The Weight of Wonder

A snail carries its home so slow,
While pondering what it doesn't know.
With every inch, it thinks and sighs,
What if the garden is full of lies?

A toddler asks, with eyes so bright,
"Why can't we fly with all our might?"
I laugh and say, "As far as we go,
There's always more that we just don't know."

A tree stands tall, it cannot speak,
Yet in its rings, life's secrets peek.
With every storm, it bends and waves,
Showing us how wonder saves.

In the end, we chuckle wide,
At all the things we cannot hide.
For in the weight of pondered cheer,
We find the joy that keeps us near.

A Journey Through Enigma

When I find my keys, it's quite the thrill,
Only to lose them, oh what a drill!
Where's the milk? Oh no, it's not on the shelf,
Perhaps it's hiding, like a shy little elf.

Why do socks vanish in the wash's embrace?
Do they party in folds, just out of place?
I asked my shoe, but it just squeaked,
Guess it's a secret that I mustn't peek.

Spilled my cereal, what a grand mess,
How did the cat get involved, I confess?
I ponder the weather, with umbrella in hand,
Only to find the sun's made a stand.

Each question I ask leads to more fun,
Do fish ever wonder if they can run?
As I stumble through riddles and playful blurs,
I laugh with each answer, my mind spins like furs.

Cascades of Curiosity

Why do cats sit in boxes so tight?
Is it because they think it's all right?
My plants plot revenge, or so it seems,
As they start to wilt, killing my dreams.

Do pancakes flip back and forth with glee?
Or do they wish they could float carefree?
As I stack them high, they whisper a tune,
Perhaps I should question the fork and the spoon.

Is pizza a pie, or something divine?
With each cheesy slice, how do I define?
Do creatures above laugh while watching us roam?
Or do they just think that we're far from home?

Each smile a puzzle, each giggle a clue,
I tackle the absurd, oh what can we do?
Through puzzles and wonders, we chase after mirth,
Finding joy in the chaos, we dance on this Earth.

The Echo of Yesterday

Why did I walk into that room alone?
Just to forget what I clearly have known?
My forgetful brain makes silly demands,
Like asking my left for the right with my hands.

Yesterday's lunch is a fading delight,
Leftover pizza? Or was it a kite?
I ponder the flavors as I munch with care,
Did that broccoli wave, or was it a glare?

The clock ticks slowly; what is the phase?
Am I stuck in a time loop? Oh, how it sways!
With each tick and tock, I juggle my thoughts,
Trying to remember the lessons I've fought.

Finding humor in failure, a twist of fate,
Was the answer hiding? Or just too late?
With echoes of laughter, I wade through the day,
Wondering if onions too, have things to say.

Paths Woven in Doubt

Steps forward lead me in circles, it's clear,
Why does my GPS want me to steer?
I followed the path that it laid out for me,
Only to question if I'll pee on a tree.

Who picked the color for that blinking sign?
Wait, did I just pass it? Oh, that can't be fine.
Maps in my pocket, but a twist of fate,
Leaves me confused, stuck in wild debate.

Why do we run when we can just stroll?
Should we ride on a duck or simply a shoal?
With laughter and joy, I ponder the way,
Finding new trails like a child in play.

As choices unfold in peculiar ways,
I dance through the confusion on wobbly balays.
Paths woven with wonder, a funny game,
Each turn is a smile, nothing feels the same.

www.ingramcontent.com/pod-product-compliance
Lightning Source LLC
Chambersburg PA
CBHW051637160426
43209CB00004B/687